# 1000 Words or Bust
## How to Survive and Thrive as a Freelance Writer

Michelle L. Slaton

Copyright © 2014 Michelle L. Slaton

All rights reserved.

ISBN-10: 1494773562
ISBN-13: 978-1494773564

DEDICATION

To Janie Francis Waddell
Your unwavering love and support are priceless - as are you.

## CONTENTS

| | Acknowledgments | i |
|---|---|---|
| 1 | So You Want To Be A Freelance Writer | 1 |
| 2 | Time Stands Still For No Writer | 4 |
| 3 | Enter The Internet | 7 |
| 4 | Social Media Is Your Friend | 12 |
| 5 | The Shop Is Open | 14 |
| 6 | You Are All Write | 15 |
| 7 | Resource List | 17 |

## ACKNOWLEDGMENTS

A huge THANK YOU to my readers. This process would not be nearly as thrilling for me without you. I welcome your thoughts, comments, suggestions, and questions. Please mail me directly at 1000wordsorbust@gmail.com or visit www.michelle-ink.com and we can begin a conversation there.

*Cover image courtesy of stockimages at www.FreeDigitalPhotos.net*

# 1 SO YOU WANT TO BE A FREELANCE WRITER

You want to be a freelance writer and I am going to tell you how to go about doing it. I am not going to sugarcoat the process, lie, or lead you down a path of misinformation. I will put the information you need here in as concise a manner as possible so as not to waste your time because believe me, you are going to need every minute you have to get in as much writing as you possibly can.

This will not be anywhere near the length of a novel or even a short story. It does not need to be. A bit of direction and resources will get you well on your way to starting your professional freelance writing career.

First things first. You do not need any formal college training to be a freelance writer. Do not send any money to anyone for writing seminars or freelance workshops, etc. My book, your good sense, and raw talent are more than enough to get you well on your way to freelancing.

You obviously feel you have the knack for writing and I am not going to second guess your choice. You are also probably very much aware that there will be some marketing and self-selling that will have to be done. You are up to it.

## The Basics

I am going on a couple of assumptions here concerning your

writing set-up. I assume you are using a computer to work on and that you have a reliable connection to the Internet. You also have a word processing program you are familiar with. If you do not have this particular kind of software, there are several good ones out there available for purchase depending on what platform your computer operates on, i.e., Windows, OS X, or GNU/Linux to name the big boys.

There is an excellent one available for free that allows you to produce high quality output comparable to the commercial programs on the market. It is called Open Office Writer and you will need to download it from the Internet. It is packaged as an office suite, meaning there is additional software programs bundled together with it that you might find handy to have. Visit www.openoffice.org to get yourself a copy. They have a very active community and many resources to help you learn the ins and outs of Open Office.

I am also assuming that you have examined this endeavor from all sides and planned accordingly. Are you going to pursue this goal on a full-time basis? Is it feasible for you to go without an income for possibly weeks at a time? Are there any travel plans around the corner? (Have laptop, will travel.) Any plans for company coming for a bit of a stay? Do you have any health issues that you have scheduled to be taken care of? These are all things you need to analyze, acknowledge, and plan around accordingly.

**Where There's a Will**

We have addressed the things you don't need to have, the preplanning, and the physical tools that will make the writing process possible. Now we are moving on to what you must have that only you can supply. No book or piece of software can give you the one element every successful freelance writer has to have - unlimited determination. I cannot stress enough how pivotal this one trait will be. You will find out for yourself, this I promise you my friend.

It may sound like a cliché but this does not make it any less true. Ask any successful person and they will tell you that what set them up for success more than anything else was the ability to soldier on despite the obstacles. Nothing in this life worth having is obtained easily - for the most part.

Should you find yourself in a bit of a slump, uninspired, frustrated, and with visions of a sledgehammer being forcefully applied to your laptop, well - time for a bit of a break! One, it happens to every writer and two, it's a perfect reason to play hooky. Go for a walk or a drive. Plunge yourself amidst the masses. Every time your thoughts stray back to writing, gently chase them away. In no time at all, you will be surprised how soon, inspiration will strike.

The longer you write and the more different types of writing you create will give you just that much more confidence in yourself. You will be surprised as well about the things you will learn, not just in regards to the craft of writing but also the subject matter you will be researching and writing about.

You already know the many benefits working as a freelance writer offers you; from setting your own hours, working from home, being your own boss - to having the flexibility to work wherever you, your computer, and the Internet can meet up. Once you sell your first piece of work, there will be no stopping you and the times you doubted yourself will be long forgotten.

**Searching High and Low**

Once your freelance writing career takes off, you may be working on several projects at one time. It will be extremely important for you to stay organized.

Nothing is more aggravating than having to perform a search on your entire hard disk because you never got around to creating logical folders to put different projects in.

You will also find after submitting voluminous amounts of bid proposals that potential clients may go weeks or months before they award you the job. If you do not stay organized, you will have a hard time saving face if you must have your "memory refreshed."

Finally, you will find no two clients are the same when it is time to get paid. Keeping up with who pays by the hour, page, word, or project is an important detail. How they want invoices submitted, yet another important detail.

You will be doing yourself a huge favor by becoming organized and staying that way.

## 2 TIME STANDS STILL FOR NO WRITER

    The biggest skill any writer can have, aside from innate talent, is managing time wisely. Writing can be soothing. Writing can transport you hundreds of miles away. Writing can carry you along until before you know it, the clock says 4:20 a.m.
    After you have gotten a few work assignments behind you, you will quickly find that if you do not manage your time, writing jobs, and other responsibilities that take you away from writing (the horror) well, you will quickly find yourself in a bit of a bind. You will not be the first author to do so either - not that I know anything about that.
    There is an idiom that applies to writing and I want you to burn it into your brain cells. It is called the five Ps and goes something like this: Prior Planning Prevents Perfectly Poor Performance. So simple and so true.
    Having said that, time to sit down and put pen to paper. I am suggesting a brainstorm party of epic proportions. You are going to need a timer, alarm clock, or you can use the alarm on your cell phone. Your timeframe - two minutes. Grab about four sheets of paper to write on and then place these titles at the top of a those pages, one per page. I enjoy writing about _____ the most. I have wanted to write about _____ but never got the chance. I am very good; maybe even an expert, at _____. I have always wanted to know about/learn how to _____.
    Now, take a break. Visit the kitchen, restroom, etc. Walk the

dog if applicable. Put your phone on flight mode. Make yourself comfortable, take a deep breath, set your timer/alarm for two minutes and write anything and everything applicable to the title at the top of the paper that comes to mind. Write until the alarm goes off. If you should get stumped at some point, just start writing verbs and nouns down. Once you finish one page, turn it over, take about a minute to clear your mind, stretch, and then start again.

Why did I have you do this? You just saved yourself a great deal of time by coming up with topics to write about. It was also an exercise in self-appraisal. Realizing your strengths allows you to focus on them instead of wasting time concerned about your weaknesses.

Get in the habit of makings lists. Before your work day is over, make a list of tasks you want to complete the following day. Then, as you knock out each item on the list, cross it off. You will be surprised at how much you can accomplish and by tackling each task separately, you will not feel so stressed.

If you have a large writing project you have undertaken, making a list of the different aspects can be a great help. Taking a large endeavor and breaking it down in to smaller and more manageable pieces can greatly reduce any anxiety you might have. Checking off the completed items will give you an awesome feeling of accomplishment.

Acquire a calendar you can write on. I suggest the kind that comes in book form that you can keep near at hand. If you have things due on a certain day, mark them on the calendar the day before. Regularly look at your calendar, glance at the next month to keep an eye on the upcoming projects you have lined up. You can, of course, handle this via electronic means. I have found, for myself, that the act of writing an event down and then physically opening my calendar and looking at it helps me remember better. Plus, having the calendar on my desk serves as a visual prompt for me.

Keep a journal or sticky notes nearby as well so you can jot down ideas as they come to mind. Many times you will be working on one particular project when out of the blue, you have a brilliant idea. There are some free sticky note programs available for free. You can download an excellent one from here: http://www.hottnotes.com.

The next chapter is going to give you tips on using the Internet to help you as you start writing freelance. The Internet is a great tool for communication, research, and marketing. It can also be a huge time-waster. You can easily find yourself perusing through pictures of cute kittens when about 30 clicks ago, you were busy researching your next article topic. Again, not that this has ever happened to me you understand.

# 3 ENTER THE INTERNET

You will discover when you first begin this journey that you will spend a good bit of time in the beginning finding work. No, you will not be running out and going door to door, business cards in hand, to all your local businesses. There is no picking up of the phone and cold calling. Your freelance job search will be strictly via the Internet.

Unless you just want to do those things and you certainly can. A visit to your local printing companies, newspapers, and any others you think might be good contacts for you, will certainly not be wasted time or effort. I applaud your industry if you do, myself, I am a hermit hence the freelance ghost writing gig. While you are at it, let your neighbors, hair stylist, dentist, family and friends, the clerk at the gas station, the bank teller (I think you get the idea); know that you are now a freelance writer.

My point being, before I digressed, is that there is a world of opportunity online if you just know how to go about finding it. You are already several steps ahead in the game since I am going to tell you where it is.

**The World Goes...Web**

Advances in technology have greatly improved how we live, work, and play. The Internet has made the world a much smaller place. Communicating with a potential client in India takes just a few clicks of the mouse. Services like PayPal have made the accounts payable and accounts receivable aspects of doing business as a highly professional freelance writer such as yourself much more secure and convenient.

## Elance.com and oDesk.com

Elance.com and oDesk.com are two websites whose services are greatly under-utilized. Do not get me wrong, the competition on both sites is fierce but there is still plenty of work to go around. Both of these websites put clients and freelancers in touch with one another.

They are both free to post jobs on, create profiles for, and apply and submit projects through. They do charge a small fee at the time of payment but for the service you are receiving, it is well worth it.

You are not going to get rich but what you are going to get, especially as a shiny new freelance writer, is valuable experience, a body of work, and exposure to opportunities. They both offer you the ability to test your skills and depending on how you do, you can post the results on your profile (if you do not do as well as you would have liked, you have the option of keeping the results off your profile and after a waiting period, you can retest).

When creating your profile, take the time to be thorough and create a professional presence for yourself on each site. Upload a picture and complete your entire profile - it takes some time but will serve you well.

You will be able to create a portfolio to showcase your work. "But wait, I just started out, I do not have a portfolio yet," you say to yourself. Remember the brainstorming we did earlier in the book? Take the page titled along the lines of "I am Very Good; Maybe Even an Expert at _____" and pick two of those items you wrote down. Create a 500 word informative and interesting article about each. There you go, two samples of your work you can upload and refer to when you start bidding on jobs. Of course, you want to check, re-check, and triple check these articles because they are shouting out to one and all about the quality of work you produce.

Here are a couple of tips about both of these sites. You have to remember that you are going to be conversing with people from around the world. For many, English is going to be a second language for them. This will require you to be extra careful when explaining yourself. Do not get impatient with someone if you have to correspond back and forth several times to ensure everyone is on the same page.

Never plagiarize, i.e., copy someone else's work. There is a nifty website called Copyscape.com that will catch you every time and clients use it, often. Never lie about your experience or ability in order to obtain a job. Be patient, it is not worth earning a bad reputation and jeopardizing your ability to use either service to gain experience and a source of income.

Never let a potential client talk you into submitting an original work as a "test" to be considered for a project unless you are going to be paid for it. Not that I would know anything about that. And yes, I have utilized both websites myself.

## Ezine Article Directories

Should you decide to freelance on Elance.com or oDesk.com you will see that a good many webmasters hire freelance writers to create original and fresh content for their websites. They are hiring writers to work as "ghost" writers. This simply means that you write the article and the client will publish it under their own name. You give up all rights and claims to the article and should you try to resell or publish the article; you can be prosecuted for breach of copyright.

Another use for eZine Article Directories is they serve as an excellent form of advertising for you, the freelance writer and while you do not typically get paid, you also do not have to pay for the traffic that is generated to your website (we shall look at why you should have a website of you own in a later chapter).

How this generally works is you create a 350-500 word article, try to keep it under 500 words, and upload it to an eZine directory. You may have to register on the directory but there should be no charges involved. Each eZine will have its own criteria for publishing, from word count to format. Along with the article, you will be presented with the option of creating either a resource box or author bio. The resource box and bio are your free forms of advertising. You may be limited to 3 or 5 lines of text but that should still give you plenty of room to enter a brief description of your services, an email address, and your website information.

**Research Papers/Essays**

Students can also be a source of work for you. They will pay fairly good money for an essay or research paper. In order to do this kind of writing, you will need to be familiar with both APA and MLA formatting. (I will furnish a list at the end of the book that will have an invaluable amount of resources to point you to on the Internet).

You can advertise your services on a website like Craigslist.com. You will not have anywhere near the bulk of opportunity you would have on either Elance.com or oDesk.com, however, earn that one student an A and he will tell his friends who in turn will tell their friends, and so on.

**Why You Will Love Google**

Spend some time with a writer's best friend, Google. Google will make your life as a freelance writer so much easier. It is indispensable as a research tool and you will spend a good bit of time doing just that, research.

Believe it or not, indirectly Google will help support your freelance writing career. How so? A little thing called search engine optimization (SEO).

SEO simply means trying to get a website as high as possible on Google and Bing search-results pages; it is a part of the webmaster's marketing and growth strategy. The proper use of SEO should result in more traffic to a website. This is why webmasters are willing to pay ghost writers for original, creative, and fresh content for their websites, inadvertently creating work for you, the professional freelance writer.

**Interest Groups and Forums**

The next chapter is going to touch on how social media can help the aspiring freelance writer and it would seem like a more fitting place for this subject matter to appear. However, I included it under our Internet discussion because there are so many different writing blogs, forums, chat rooms, and websites specifically aimed at writers.

These websites offer more than just merely networking, which of course they do, but many of them are additionally great resources for the craft of writing itself. They offer instruction in the proper use of punctuation and grammar and tips on writing style.

They hold writing competitions often and for just about every skill level and genre. These communities of writers are generous with their skills and can be very powerful in bringing attention to causes they believe in.

Freelance writing can often be a solitary occupation. Many of us love this about writing. There are others among us though that are much more socially adept and utilize forums quite a bit to meet and converse with friends, old and new.

# 4 SOCIAL MEDIA IS YOUR FRIEND

This makes perfect sense since of course 98% of the work you will be doing is going to be generated by the Internet. I am going to discuss how Twitter, Google+, and Facebook can enable you to gain valuable advertising - for free. I am assuming you are somewhat familiar with these and will not go into a tutorial on how to use them.

**TWITTER**

Since its debut, there have been over 163 billion tweets published. That is a staggering amount. To say that Twitter is a popular social medium would be an understatement.

Here is another statistic that goes a long way for jumping on the Twitter bandwagon; 73% of U.S. online consumers trust information and advice from Twitter. Because tweets are so limited in size (140 characters) you will not spend so much time keeping up with you Twitter account.

**FACEBOOK**

Facebook is another social media tool and not only do you have the ability to create your very own Facebook page, but you may also create one for your writing endeavors.

You ultimately want your name to appear as often as possible when folks perform a web search and the more websites you utilize, the better your chances are for this.

## GOOGLE+

Google+ is another social media site that will prove priceless. Not only will you be able to acquire a free email account but you are able to integrate all the Google products and Google Drive is a great medium on which to share your work while freeing up memory on your computer. Free is always a good price to have to pay for a new writer just beginning their career.

## A WEBSITE

I also suggest that you look into starting your own website. Not only does it give your current and prospective clients a means to reach you, it also lends you more credibility. There are several sites where you can purchase a domain name. You can pay by the month, year or even by ten years. The longer you pay for your domain, the higher you will appear in Google search results.

Once you have your domain name, you will need to find a web hosting company and there are several to choose from. As with the domain name, you have options for the length of time you can pay for, be it monthly, semi-annually or annually.

## 5 THE SHOP IS NOW OPEN

You have all your bases covered by now, except one. You have to be able to get paid after all. I suggest utilizing PayPal. It is a free service and it seems to be the one that the majority of people use.

Another thing to keep in mind as far as payment is there are unscrupulous people out there. If you take on a large project, ask for a retainer and never submit any work to "prove" yourself. The topic they may have you write about might very well be the material they are looking for and they just got it for free.

Once you have completed an assignment, ask your client if they would be willing to write a testimonial for you along with having their picture appear on your website or other Internet presence. Most people are more than willing to help you out.

Shop around and determine the most affordable way to get yourself some business cards. You can create some yourself until you can afford a higher quality. Always carry a supply of them with you; you never know when an opportunity will present itself.

I also recommend magnets for your car. They are a one-time investment that will pay for themselves ten times over.

Once your writing takes off and you are earning a fairly regular profit, I suggest having some other promotional items made up. These can include personalized ink pens, calendars, post-it notes - be creative! The whole point is to give your business as much exposure as possible. Vistaprint.com is a very reasonable website that produces quality promotional goods.

You will find that a lot of people utilize Skype to communicate. It is a free service and for a fee, you can acquire your own phone number. Speaking of phone numbers, make certain to edit you voicemail to reflect your new freelance writing services.

# 6 YOU ARE ALL WRITE

The last subject I am going to touch upon is perhaps the most important - your mindset. You are a professional freelance writer, an author, and entrepreneur.

You are embarking on an endeavor that most people only dream about. It can be a scary proposition but the benefits will far outweigh the anxiety once you get yourself under way.

The great thing about freelance writing is there is not much start-up expense involved. Writing is one of those things that is only limited by your imagination.

If you find yourself stuck on one project, set it aside and work on another. Often you will find inspiration can strike when you least expect it and it is usually those "ah ha" moments that can make all the difference in the world.

You have heard the expression "fake it until you make it." That is absolutely true. When you think about it, there is a fine line between having works published and actively working to sell your writing. Remaining positive is extremely important

Once you are able to start your own website, start a blog and this way you can refer potential clients to your work and they can get a better idea of your writing style. Whatever you do, do NOT give up. As I said in the very beginning of this ebook, determination separates the successful from the wannabes.

To begin with, figure out what your niche is. You will be inspired to write more and your exuberance will come through in your writing. Are you an expert at investing? Or perhaps card games? Maybe romance novels or science fiction let you showcase your imagination.

Set aside a portion of each day to do some writing. It doesn't have to be hours on end. You know how the writing process can be. Once you start and hit a stride, the material will seem to flow effortlessly.

Thank you for purchasing this ebook. I hope that you can utilize the advice contained in it to get yourself up and running. I know I certainly could have benefited from such book. If you have any comments or suggestions, please contact me at michellelslaton@michelle-ink.com. I am always willing to help a fellow writer out.

The resources I mentioned in the book begin on the next page. I will gladly answer any questions you might have about any of them. I wish you nothing but every success.

# 7 RESOURCE LIST

The following list contains all those resources I mentioned in the text of the book. You will not be able to find a more concise and useful guide for freelance writing tools in one place.

**Open Office software program**
www.openoffice.org

**Free sticky notes program**
www.hottnotes.com

**Online staffing platforms**
www.elance.com
www.odesk.com

**Promotional items - business cards, calendars, etc.**
www.vistaprinta.com

**Google SEO Guide**
http://static.googleusercontent.com/media/www.google.com/en/us/webmasters/docs/search-engine-optimization-starter-guide.pdf

**Free communication service, includes video, texting, and phone services**
   www.skype.com

**Payment service**
   www.paypal.com

**Ezine Article Directory**
   http://www.ezinearticlespedia.com

**MLA formatting guidelines**
   https://owl.english.purdue.edu/owl/resource/747/01/

**APA formatting guidelines**
   http://www.apastyle.org/

ABOUT THE AUTHOR

Michelle L. Slaton was born in Greenville, SC in 1970. She has had an affinity for writing her entire life and finally indulged in her one true calling in 2000 and has not looked back. She is a published poet, author, and ghost writer. She enjoys writing, reading, and haunting the Internet. Michelle and her doggy daughter, Flossie Mae, live on the east coast of the United States.

www.ingramcontent.com/pod-product-compliance
Lightning Source LLC
Chambersburg PA
CBHW051829170526
45167CB00005B/2209